Library of
Davidson College

THE BEST BLOOD

OF THE COUNTRY

BOOKS BY GEORGE KEITHLEY

The Best Blood of the Country
Earth's Eye
The Burning Bear
To Bring Spring
Scenes from Childhood
Song in a Strange Land
The Donner Party
Themes in American Literature, *Co-Editor*

THE BEST BLOOD

OF THE COUNTRY

George Keithley

Mellen Poetry Press
Lewiston/Queenston/Lampeter

Library of Congress Cataloging-in-Publication Data

Keithley, George, 1935-
    The best blood of the country / George Keithley.
       p. cm.
    ISBN 0-7734-2766-X
    1. Burr, Aaron, 1756-1836--Drama. 2. Burr Conspiracy, 1805-1807--Fiction. 3. Burr-Hamilton Duel, Weehawken, N.J., 1804--Drama.
4. United States--History--1801-1809--Drama. I. Title.
PS3561.E378B46   1993
812'.54--dc20   92-44217
                                                                     CIP

Copyright © 1993 George Keithley.
All rights reserved. Author inquiries and orders:

Mellen Poetry Press
The Edwin Mellen Press
P. O. Box 450
Lewiston, New York 14092

Printed in the United States of America

For Mike and Merrie McLaughlin

"Suppose you were looking for damned men among the American dead. . . damned men whose damnation would have meaningful modern significance. . . Would you include Burr—not for his undoubted treason, or his apparently cold-blooded execution of Hamilton, but for that so-modern combination of viciousness and charm?"
—Archibald MacLeish

"No apologies. I despise them!"
—Aaron Burr

Acknowledgments

Selected as a finalist in the National Poetry Series competition, the Charlotte Repertory Theatre's Festival of New American Plays, the Dayton Repertory Theatre competition, and the Permian Basin Theatre Contest, *The Best Blood of the Country* has won first prize in the DramaRama festival of new plays, sponsored by the Playwrights' Center of San Francisco, and first prize in the Duke Players Playwriting Contest, sponsored by Duke University. It also has received the Leighton Rollins Award for verse drama, presented by the New England Poetry Club.

> Act I, Scene 2, was first published in *Crazyquilt,* and
> Act I, Scene 3, in the long-poem issue of *Porch.*

> Act II was first published in *The North American Review.*

> Act III, Scene 1, first appeared in *The Reaper,* and
> Act III, Scenes 2 and 4, in *The University Journal.*

> "A Drama of Living Forms" originally appeared in *The Reaper.*

The statement by Archibald MacLeish appears in *Letters of Archibald MacLeish,* edited by R.H. Winnick... A concert reading from *The Best Blood of the Country* has been presented at California State University, Chico. The Playwrights' Center of San Francisco presented the first staged reading of the play at Fort Mason in San Francisco. Subsequently, a staged reading has been presented at the Foothill Writers Conference in Los Altos Hills, California.

Contents

Preface	7
Act I	13
Act II	45
Act III	65
A Drama of Living Forms	107

Preface

In the years following the American Revolution, Aaron Burr believes that the best and boldest spirit in the country is his own. Bristling with ambition, he first gained fame in the Revolution by his daring, his bravery under fire, and his disregard for the orders of commanding officers. Although Burr was heroic on the battlefield, General Washington found him unfit for promotion because of his avid ambition. However others might judge him, he sees himself always in the role of a hero. His idol is Napoleon, and he craves the esteem of all the world.

Alexander Hamilton is as eager for martyrdom as Burr is for power and glory. He brings to politics the desperate energy of a life-or-death struggle.

Older than both his rivals, Thomas Jefferson seeks the ideal of a community of individuals, the paradox of freedom and responsibility; a balance always difficult to sustain in the political storm of the moment.

A descendant of the Puritan churchman Jonathan Edwards, Burr is an agnostic and a relentless womanizer. He was a devoted husband and father, and he advocated educational, social, and political opportunity for women, convinced their contributions would improve the world. Yet he preys upon women, always pursuing what he calls, in his private letters, a conquest.

Throughout his turbulent life Burr remained guarded (enemies said *calculating*), and a number of his letters are written in code, even to his family and close friends. For a public figure he's an intensely private man, a trait which contributes to many rumors and suspicions which circulate about him. And to provoke the suspicious mind still further, he shares none of Jefferson's ideal of society or the citizen.

Burr argues that he must be free to use his talent to its full potential. But his intrigues to gain power cannot fulfill his inner life.

He will sometimes tire of his hunger for admiration, and wonder why humanity is unhappy. Why the one creature that claims to rule all this planet is unable to enjoy it. When the drama darkens, remorse broods in Burr. But doubt and guilt do not. He once confided to his daughter Theo that had he died, "The poor world would have been deprived of the heir-apparent to all its admiration and glory."

Writing *In the American Grain*, William Carlos Williams wisely suspected the motives of Burr's accusers, chiefly Hamilton and Jefferson; they had much to gain by maligning him. Williams further argued: "Perhaps Burr carried into politics an element of democratic government, even a major element, those times were slighting. . . an element so powerful and so rare that he was hated for it, feared—and loved." That rare element is the total liberty of a free individual, as it manifests itself in the imagination and in action. This virtue that Williams sees in Burr is truly a virtue in Williams, and that's why he sees it. But to see it in Burr he has to ignore Burr's own words and deeds which often testify to his cunning, his distrust of democracy, and his desire for fame and wealth, which are the motives for many of his actions. It's a hard case to make. Yet Williams is right to say that Burr champions individual liberty, and for this he <u>was</u> hated, feared, and loved. There may be no better summary of Burr's life than what Williams wrote of him: "The world is made to eat, not leave, that the spirit may be full, not empty."

Act I depicts the struggle between Burr and Jefferson in the election of 1801. Burr has bribed his way onto the ballot as Jefferson's running-mate. Frankly ambitious, he boasts that he seeks glory, and he stalks it at any cost. Now he'll try to take the office of President for himself, and the country must choose between Burr's absolute independence and Jefferson's quest for a democratic community.

Act II brings to its climax Burr's struggle with Hamilton. The duel they'd rehearsed as rivals in the army, in law courts, in love, in politics, must now be fought. But if the question of suicide isn't raised, the duel makes little sense. Why did Hamilton accept Burr's challenge? For years he'd known Burr was the superior marksman.

Hamilton's skills in the army were political--a fact that Burr bitterly resented--wherease Burr's talent with a pistol was often noted, and target-shooting was his favorite recreation. Hamilton's friends argued that his honor compelled him to fight the duel, but how honorable was his conduct which had provoked it? It's tempting to think he is history's noble victim. The truth is that he forms his own fate, and he hopes to gain from the outcome of the duel something extraordinary and eternal.

Act III reveals Burr's conspiracy to conquer the territory west of the Appalachians, and all of Mexico, to gain an empire which he intends to rule. Never an advocate of Jefferson's republic, Burr knows his aim is solitary when he launches the conspiracy that leads to his arrest. A hero in the Revolution, elected to the Senate, later Vice President, a man who nearly was elected President over Thomas Jefferson; now he is to stand trial for treason. However, not even the influence of the President can determine the verdict. Burr is to be tried, ultimately, in the conscience of his countrymen.

That conscience is conveyed by the Workers Chorus, people Burr brought into political life by way of Tammany Hall. Because there can be no democracy without them, they appear everywhere, delivering their opinions while they work, changing the sets, providing transition. Often they speak in rhyme, suggesting they share a common judgement. More than once their doggerel urges us to consider events from a public viewpoint. It reminds us that we're hearing the popular opinion about Burr or the events surrounding him. And if he abandons these people, they must demonstrate their disenchantment with a man who pursues power not to enrich their lives after all, but to appease his anxious soul.

The Cast

AARON BURR. In his mid-forties, Burr is short, nimble, quick in mind and body. Dark hair recedes from a prominent forehead; large coal-dark eyes; delicate features. His manner is courtly, elaborate. In public he always plays to an audience, and his speech is emphatic, intended to make a point.

THEODOSIA. Burr's daughter is young, quick-witted, a stunning beauty with dark red hair, fair complexion. Intelligent and a little ribald, she's encouraged in both qualities by her father.

THOMAS JEFFERSON. Twelve years older than Burr, he has a soft voice and his hair is full but grey. His costume is usually casual. Keenly intelligent, he's also shrewd, and firm of purpose. Sometimes aloof, especially around Burr.

ALEXANDER HAMILTON. In his mid-forties, he is fair, trim, handsome. A man of sharp tongue and firm convictions, he fears democracy will lead to tyranny. In politics he's an unscrupulous opponent, yet he remains a gracious figure. Often fiery, at times melancholy, he cares passionately about the political struggle in which he is engaged.

DOLLEY MADISON. At thirty-three she is self-assured, intelligent, and very sociable. She has a 'sweet' face, wears her dark hair high; she's a little buxom, and in the fashion of the time she favors low-cut, pretty gowns. An accomplished charmer, she has many admirers, including Burr.

JOHN MARSHALL. An astute politician in his mid-forties, the Chief Justice is tall, handsome, and he carries his responsibilities comfortably. He has no love for Jefferson. Fellow Virginians, they're separated by politics and personality. Marshall is affable; he enjoys a party, conversation, and drinking with a friend, such as Burr.

WORKERS CHORUS. A freed slave, a brick layer, a clerk, and a longshoreman. They're solid, spirited men, proud to be the work force of the new world. Speaking frankly, often in doggerel, they provide public opinion about Burr. And they make the necessary set changes, remaining in character as workers while performing their tasks before the audience.

BETSY BOWEN. A high-spirited courtesan, she is younger than Burr or Hamilton, and pursued by both. Clearly independent, she knows her way around the men who think they make use of her.

SALLY HEMINGS. A young black woman in Jefferson's household, she is reluctant to speak to anyone but him. She is ever watchful, attentive.

LAWYER PERKINS. A tall, raw-boned country lawyer; strong and clever. A man of independent thought and action.

WILLIAM LOVE. Young, fastidious, conservative, he is loyal to his employer, who owns the island where Burr assembles his army. He will be a witness for the prosecution.

A VOICE. (later **A JUROR**). A working man in the audience calls out questions during Burr's trial, then comes on stage to give the verdict.

GENERAL JAMES WILKINSON. Portly, red-faced, white-haired, he's a double traitor who struts his importance to hide his shame.

THE BEST BLOOD

OF THE COUNTRY

ACT ONE

Scene 1

Examining a pair of pistols, BURR stands near the small table which serves as his desk. A globe is close by. His coat is red velvet and his boots are highly polished. He'll wear the two pistols at his belt. Always performing, he commands attention.

In one doorway JEFFERSON waits, holding a sheet of paper. He wears a dark blue outfit with white ruffled sleeves.

A party is in progress in the house. A second door, to the left, is closed. On the table downstage are cups, glasses, a wine decanter, candles. Several plain chairs flank this table and there's a chair by the desk.

BURR.
Mr. Jefferson, I asked you to my home
for the pleasure of your company.

JEFFERSON.
And not to test your weapons, Colonel Burr?

BURR *(in good humor).*
We did hold a target shoot on the lawn.

JEFFERSON *(approaching).*
Which you must have won, Aaron.

BURR *(as he puts the pistols in his belt).*
Happily, I defeated Hamilton.
His tongue does more damage than his guns.

JEFFERSON *(handing BURR the sheet of paper).*
He's the evil genius of this country.

BURR.
Are you our guardian angel?

JEFFERSON *(laughs softly).*
Oh, no. But look at our latest tally—
Colonel, we control the necessary votes.

BURR *(with a glance at the paper).*
Your election is as certain as my aim.
Remember, this was my prediction
when I became your running-mate.

JEFFERSON.
As to that—

BURR.
Sir?

JEFFERSON.
You left me little choice.

BURR *(waving the paper at him).*
I promised my men would deliver New York.
Without this state, Tom,
you could no more hope to be President
than the Pope. Your choice was clear:
Put Burr on your ticket or retire to your farm.

JEFFERSON.
You think I owe my election to your name?

BURR *(slaps the paper on the desk).*
You know damn well it's true.
And I'll be Vice President thanks to you.

JEFFERSON.
Colonel, we've made a strange marriage.
I hope we may keep a quiet house.

BURR.
That's your pleasure.

JEFFERSON.
A pleasure, no, but it *is* my desire
to create that community
where an individual lives in liberty
and accepts responsibility
for the state. This land and its laws.
Here we stand at arm's reach

and we dare not touch hands like friends—
Are we already a world apart?

BURR *(lifts the globe from its stand).*
We *are* an unlikely pair, you and I.
Still we share one desire—
To grasp this globe like a tot's toy.

> *He twirls the globe in his hands.*

And now the world awaits our pleasure!
For it whirls whichever way we spin it. . .

> BURR *tosses the globe to* JEFFERSON.

JEFFERSON *(setting the globe on its stand).*
I don't fancy that hollow ball.
I tell you, sir, pure and simple:
All power rests in the people.
You scoff at this ideal, but I believe
it's the heart's hot blood
in the body politic. People endure
poverty, hunger, war. For what?
Men and women sense today
the power of a prepared mind
to turn the earth to our own purpose.

> JEFFERSON *touches his temples.*

This is the world that we must map—

> *He touches* BURR'S *head in the same manner.*

Here is the miracle of humankind—

> BURR *steps back.* JEFFERSON *holds out his hands toward the globe.*

Hands no more confined to work
the king's fields, or feed his face.
First we free the human form,
then the mind is free to alter
earth and our unhappy history
we've painted over all this sphere.
We must share our hope and labor
for the human community. But you,
Colonel, despise equality—

I see difficulty for the country
in our coupling. More than one citizen
who's pledged his vote to me, will withhold it from you.

BURR.
Second-in-command is no disgrace.
It's honor enough to serve my President
as his right hand.

JEFFERSON.
Honor is all it will be. Aaron,
our vote is the public voice.
It whispers mistrust in your name.
A famous name I must strike from my list—

BURR *(impatient)*.
You keep me from my own festivities.
Sir, speak plainly.

JEFFERSON.
I can't appoint you to my cabinet.

BURR.
Oh, this is cold and clear as the winter air!
But I see clean through it.
Vice President, with no role in the government?
Ridiculous! Could defeat be worse?
Tom, when you take office all the world
will honor you. What do you fear from Burr?

JEFFERSON *(his hand on the globe)*.
Nothing on earth, since I have your support.

BURR *(as he sees THEO enter)*.
You have my New York as well!
However, that's a small matter.
Now I must trust you with my daughter.
Theo, please take Tom to greet our guests.

THEO *(offers her arm to JEFFERSON)*.
It will be my pleasure, Papa.

BURR *(aside)*.
But not theirs.

JEFFERSON *(as he leaves with THEO)*.
Colonel, we'll talk again.

BURR *(when they're gone)*.
Oh, you'll hear more from Burr, *that* I promise.
I'll be Lucifer lurking at your door.
The devoted servant you don't dare dismiss.

> *A loud knock on the door. Enter the WORKERS CHORUS: the freed slave, brick layer, clerk, and longshoreman all in work clothes. All are solidly for BURR at this point. CHORUS sometimes divides into pairs, A and B.*

CHORUS.
Four working men to see Colonel Burr.

BURR.
My young friends. Do sit down.

CHORUS *(as they sit)*.
Where's your daughter? Your better half?

BURR *(opening a locket)*.
She's helping Jefferson enjoy himself.

CHORUS.
She'll want to hear about her father's honor.
With all the electors chosen,
you've won as many votes as Jefferson!

BURR *(looking up)*.
Truly? I'm so close to glory?

> *CHORUS stands as THEO enters. BURR closes the locket, introducing THEO.*

My daughter, the only treasure in my vault.

THEO *(to CHORUS)*.
How kind of you to come.

> *CHORUS divides, with the globe between them. Lights dim on the left half of the stage.*

CHORUS.
Missy, can you guess our good news?

THEO.
You doubt my power to read your mind?
Why, this is no test. Women see
through men from the first light of day.
Though after dark we're at our best!

CHORUS.
The best is this: your papa may be President.

THEO.
He ought to be, if the office is worth our notice.

BURR.
Vice President won't suffice? You know
how Hamilton whines that I'm ambitious.
He'd howl if he heard Theo.

THEO.
He says you're a little Caesar, about to be born.
You must be aborted from the nation's womb!

CHORUS.
You should hear him in your drawing room—

> *Lights dim on the right half of the stage and come up on the left. CHORUS sits at the large table, drinking. BURR and THEO exit. HAMILTON, wearing glasses, enters. He begins to lecture the CHORUS while brandishing his pistol.*

HAMILTON.
Washington was unwilling to promote him.
So Burr withdrew from the war
to *forge* his fortune at the bar.
There he'll resort to any melodrama
to bemuse a jury and confound the court.

CHORUS.
What's the point of this to us?

HAMILTON.
While you smirk, remember, Colonel Burr
will bow, and smile, then slit your throat.
You think that's an idle threat?
Burr has less conscience than a cat.

CHORUS A.
You'll win no friends by smearing Burr!
He was our hero in the war—

CHORUS B.
Served us as our Senator.

HAMILTON.
Burr *serves* you? You're his slaves!

> *With his pistol HAMILTON traces the face of the freed slave.*

Damn this dusky face!
Where's the light of learning, here?
Your scowl is as coarse as coal.

CHORUS *(as they draw the freed slave away).*
Go to hell!
Burr's our brother!
Who brought us together in Tammany Hall?
Who taught us to pull in harness as a team?

HAMILTON.
Turned you into animals, you mean.
You're the cattle he beds in his barn.

CHORUS.
Election Day, we'll see who's led to slaughter.

HAMILTON *(puts down his pistol in disgust).*
Of course you're content—
Burr buys your vote with his whiskey
and more coins than you can count.

CHORUS.
Did you like us better, poor and sober?

      HAMILTON rushes in a rage at the freed slave in the CHORUS, *but the other three restrain him.*

HAMILTON.
You devils do well to worship Burr!
Your black face and his
black heart deserve each other.

      BURR *returns with* THEO, *sees the pistol on the table.*

BURR *(handing the pistol to* HAMILTON*)*.
Harsh words for your host, General.
Here's a more gentle weapon.

HAMILTON.
I regret your injury, but not my aim.

BURR.
It was always low.

HAMILTON.
Like yours, for certain ladies.

BURR.
We've courted the same women, sir, and quarreled
in court. But in politics we meet
our *common* enemy.

HAMILTON *(in agreement)*.
I fear in Tom's democracy
the dullest citizen will share power
with the few of us prepared to use it.

THEO.
Can anyone believe ability
is spooned out equally to babes at birth?

BURR.
We know it's not. And yet Jefferson
will put us at the mercy of any majority.

HAMILTON *(polishing his glasses).*
He makes mankind his model for the state.
But greed's a wolf that preys on opportunity—
It feeds and fattens and never fills.
Once we let loose that panting appetite
among the masses, you and I
are the first plump legs caught
in the jaws of Jefferson's community.

BURR *(wriggling suggestively).*
A leg, at least! Oh, let me be
a *member* of that community. . .
The *body* politic, my *ass!*

HAMILTON *(laughing, then serious)*
Burr, you're the devil's darling! Do you forget
you're still Tom's running-mate?
I've warned your workers to beware—
You're incapable of loyalty.

>   *Furious,* BURR *draws his pistols, but he returns them to his belt as* THEO *intercedes.*

THEO *(in anger, to* HAMILTON*).*
Were *you* ever in combat, in the war?

BURR *(still angry, to* HAMILTON*).*
I'm sure you drew your pay, you're a General now.
Think back to the Battle of Quebec,
when I carried *my* General, dying, on my back
through the shelling and the snow. Is it possible
you read that report, at your leisure in New York?
I need no lecture on loyalty. But I borrow
my motto from Bonaparte: "All glory to the most able."

HAMILTON.
Caesar, Napoleon, and Burr, of course!
But why is Nature so perverse?
Like a blind wet-nurse she gives her breast,
swollen with ambition, to boys of little stature.
And for *this* we call her Mother Nature?

Lights up on the whole stage as BETSY BOWEN *enters.*
HAMILTON *starts toward her, turns, makes an exaggerated bow to* BURR.

Ah, but here's her bounty. Burr, excuse me—
I'm you servant still, though you are not my master.

   HAMILTON *exits with his arm around* BETSY BOWEN.

THEO *(to her father)*.
Must you suffer his abuse?

CHORUS A *(with an awkward bow to* THEO*)*.
His words are more piss than powder—
Beg your pardon, Miss.

THEO.
Come now, I'm the Colonel's daughter.
If I could be undone by wicked talk,
I would have shamed poor Papa years ago.

BURR *(to* THEO*)*.
I speak no evil among women. Never did.
And if *any*one insults *your* honor
I'll kill the bastard in cold blood.

THEO *(laughing)*.
Keep your pistols for our entertainment, Papa.
They won't settle an election.

BURR *(picks up the paper from his desk)*.
Neither will our numbers.
Tom's about to betray us—

THEO *(as* BURR *shows her the paper)*.
These figures are false!

CHORUS.
Jefferson knows the true tally. But he lies.

BURR.
So I'll think the race is over
and be satisfied in second place—

THEO.
While he pawns the Cabinet seats for votes.

BURR.
You young workers we've welded together—
You clerks, you boys down on the dock—

CHORUS.
We found our voice by speaking as a bloc.

BURR.
You'll be Burr's army one day soon,
when our Constitution crackles into flame!

CHORUS.
Comes that time, no title's worth a damn!

THEO.
President Pisswater!... Why pursue it?

BURR.
This republic was written on paper.
Put those pages to the torch,
Congress will waft away like smoke...
People in panic will rise up at the scent,
they'll buck and bolt like a headstrong horse.
A king will climb into the saddle and seize the rein.

CHORUS A.
That's Hamilton's only hope.
He'll mount a throne
or go to his grave regretting it.

CHORUS B.
He can't conquer alone—
And the army's shot to hell!
Too little money and no morale.

BURR (*points to the Chorus*).
Veterans remember my conduct in the war.
They're as loyal to Colonel Burr as you are.

CHORUS.
We won't be ruled by Jefferson—
You buy the guns, we'll start the insurrection!

BURR.
Let that wait. Tonight we'll plot. . .

    CHORUS returns to drinking around the table as the lights dim on the left. THEO follows BURR to his desk, where he sits.

THEO.
Do I deserve your dark look?
If I'm at fault, Papa, please instruct me.

BURR *(takes out the locket, opens it).*
I grow melancholy because I miss your mother.
Often her loss leaves me at sea.
Missy, you must shine like a beacon
that beckons men from death. In all
this shadow world one light alone
persuades us of our worth—a brilliant woman.

THEO.
What's your wish?

BURR *(puts away the locket).*
You ignore our company. Go do you duty.
Exercise your intellect on men
who are proud of theirs. They'll learn
women have souls, and sense as well.
Don't droop like some fragile flower—
The Sweet Socialite, full-grown without a spine!

THEO.
I stand upon your pleasure, Papa.

BURR *(insistent).*
Stand erect, then. Pull your shoulders back
or your lungs will shrink.

THEO *(laughing).*
That's silly.

BURR *(starts up from his desk, bluffing a threat).*
A *nice* lady you are. Little nuisance!

THEO *(backing away).*
I'll be brisk as a broom, you'll see. You want
your daughter to delight you with her wit
like Dolley Madison. A woman of mind
and manners, Papa, but a flirt was well.

BURR *(sitting back).*
Indecent girl.
What have you heard about our affair?

THEO.
I tell no tales. . . Where is she tonight?

BURR.
I expect Dolley soon. And alone.
Jimmy's on a journey into farming country
to harvest votes for Jefferson.

THEO *(her finger tracing over the globe).*
If others knew you, Papa, as I do,
they'd give the weary laws of this world
into your hands, and free their own for applause.

BURR *(shakes his head).*
Nowhere on this globe are men at peace.

    Rising, he joins THEO *by the globe.*

For their own profit people tell a story
about our innocence and how guilt grew
like lush fruit on the Tree of Knowledge.
Throughout history, kings and clergy bully
simple souls to fear the sin of *Pride!*
The one virtue which should crown our glory!
Democracy is a dream, we'll see it fade
in our own time. No one questions
Why are we ruled? Instead you hear
Who shall govern? One or many? Very well.
If people find peace only on their knees,
let them bend to Burr.

BURR takes her hands in his.

          You know your father
isn't mad, Missy. I say this frankly—
By nature I was formed for admiration.

THEO *(nodding).*
I've lived so long with you
other men seem timid.

BURR.
Dull boys delight to lose their hearts
to a finer being, or beauty.
The idea of a Deity. Or one woman.
Colonel Burr was born to inspire
those sentiments, not to yield them.

He pretends a target shot.

I aim always at the highest honor.

THEO.
It's yours in good time.
Even if Tom wins a second term.

BURR.
I'm impatient with politics. I should wait
eight years? Impossible! Listen...

Circling THEO, he fills the air with whispers.

Burr, Burr, Burr... like the buzz of bees.
Everywhere, it's the first word we hear—
The second is *insurrection*.

THEO *(putting her hands in his again).*
My heart and hands are yours to command.

BURR.
All ambitions battle one another,
and you must aid me as your mother
once would do—we'll await our chance
to whisper secrets, guarding every glance.

They embrace. Exit THEO, as lights come up full.

Scene 2

>*As the party continues, the WORKERS CHORUS is drinking and miming around the table. Enter DOLLEY MADISON, who flirts with them until BURR draws her away.*

BURR.
My dear Dolley, what perversity led me
to encourage your marriage,
and forfeit a fascinating woman?

MADISON.
When you were near I fluttered like my fan.
I played the shy schoolgirl reduced to giggles.
I read philosophy and grew precocious.
Any nice deceit to earn your notice—
But your head was turned by more alluring ladies.
For all the ardor I inspired then,
I might have been a nun, kept in a convent house.

BURR.
I'd give my soul to gain entry.

MADISON.
How could that be done?

BURR *(makes the sign of the cross over her bosom).*
Pretend I'm a priest, ordered to inspect the property.

MADISON *(after they kiss).*
Be more modest.
Mr. Jefferson might see us.

BURR.
Just tonight I learned his treachery.
Your husband has his trust—
Ask Jimmy if it's true
Tom urges our voters to ignore me.

MADISON *(stepping back)*.
Why would he? If his margin
of victory is slim, Congress will select him.

BURR.
He needs nine states; I'll never surrender mine.

MADISON.
Aaron, you know him—
He won't participate in any plots.

    BURR *kisses her hand as* JEFFERSON *enters.*

BURR.
Was his timing ever worse?
I give you permission, Dolley,
to drive our philosopher to distraction.

    BURR *joins the drinking mime of the* CHORUS.

MADISON.
Our host appears unhappy—

JEFFERSON.
Yet he's pleased with his young workers.
They're a volatile element—
The anger of the young needs only one torch.

MADISON *(gaily)*.
Burr's blood is hot tonight.
Even his favorite whore is here,
primping in the parlor.
She knows how a challenge intrigues him.

JEFFERSON.
If he wins this election we'll never vote again.
Burr won't permit people to govern—
He'll hold office for life, that's his design.
Congress, too, unless a man's convicted of a crime.

CHORUS.
Congress can be sent home when they sin?
They won't last long enough to swear 'em in!

JOHN MARSHALL enters carrying a cane.

MADISON.
Shh! . . . Here's our Chief Justice.
One day he'll give you the oath of office.

JEFFERSON.
John Marshall is no judge of character.
He'd rather speak that oath to Aaron Burr.
Do we dare to sleep? . . .
Good night, Dolley, my coach draws up.

MADISON *(as JEFFERSON exits).*
Good night, dear heart.

BURR *(approaching).*
Gone away? Were we too wild?

MADISON.
You aggravate him when you entertain
his opponents in your own home.
Hamilton's hardly welcome.
Neither is Justice Marshall, in God's name!

DOLLY MADISON exits, avoiding MARSHALL. He takes a cup of wine from the table.

MARSHALL.
I see I'm too late for the target shoot.

BURR.
We stood in the snow under the elms—
This last storm froze all our trees,
the top limbs gleam like glass in the cold
moonlight. I took aim. . . *Crr-ack!*
I scored a hit and ice exploded in the air.
I told Hamilton, "It's like shooting a chandelier!"

MARSHALL.
Hamilton's here? He took part in the shoot?

BURR.
With little luck.
I invited him to be sure
he'd find enough wine to warm his tongue.

> BETSY BOWEN *enters and flirts with the* CHORUS.

BOWEN.
And a wench—

BURR.
To steal his strategy. I swear
he'll bare his heart to Betsy.

MARSHALL *(watching her)*.
Will he bare nothing else?

BURR.
They'll both *bear* watching. I'll follow her home.
He wont' be *long* with her, he has *little* to offer.

BOWEN *(approaching Burr)*.
Perhaps you sell him short.

> *Laughter from* CHORUS.

MARSHAL *(to* BURR*)*.
Tom's spies will whisper
you are intimate with his enemy.

BURR *(an arm around* BETSY BOWEN*)*.
I plead guilty, sir, to every intimacy.

MARSHALL *(as he exits)*.
How long must I wait for Hamilton to lose
his heart? Give him one hour. Not a minute more.

BOWEN *(teasing)*.
Why should I turn him out?
He's *every inch* your equal in . . . amour.

BURR.
You dare to compare us?

HAMILTON enters with THEO.

Hush! Here he is. Go to work.

The freed slave from the CHORUS brings the wine decanter and a cup to BETSY BOWEN. She pours wine for HAMILTON, then lifts the cup to his lips. His gaze follows her as BOWEN exits.

THEO.
I've captured the General here in our house—
Papa, pay ransom for his release!

BURR.
To free Hamilton from your charm? What's your price?

THEO.
A kiss.

HAMILTON.
Allow me to earn my liberty.

HAMILTON kisses THEO. Releasing him, she stands by BURR.

The girl has the nerve of her famous father.
Must you test it, sir,
by bringing blacks among your guests?

BURR.
My home is theirs, too.

THEO *(sitting).*
So is the wide world.

HAMILTON.
License like this will make it so.
Tom Jefferson's children
represent the whole color spectrum.

The freed slave from the CHORUS stand over THEO.

Burr, be prudent at home, while there's time.

BURR.
Theo's safe.
That color they wear won't rub off.

HAMILTON.
The Lord of Nature created us to mate
with our own race.

BURR *(beaming)*.
There you have the advantage of me, sir.
Never in the boudoir of a woman
was I offered His advice.

HAMILTON *(bowing)*.
God himself defers to you in these affairs.

    BETSY BOWEN *enters and beckons to* HAMILTON.

Good night, sir... My lady...
I regret my wife was too ill to share
your brilliant company. You may be sure
I'll tell her how the heavens sparkle here.

    HAMILTON *exits with* BOWEN.

THEO *(happily returns to BURR)*.
That poor man has found the ear of your courtesan
where he'll whisper his scheme
before he slips home.

BURR.
And I'll receive it later from her lips.

    Laughter from the CHORUS *as* BURR *and* THEO *exit. The* CHORUS *removes the large table and returns with a dressing screen.* BETSY BOWEN *lounges on the small bed which they wheel onstage, between the screen and the small table. Entering behind the screen,* HAMILTON *waits, half-dressed, his shirt in one hand, pistol in the other, while the* CHORUS *cries its warning to the audience.*

CHORUS A.
Latch your windows, bolt your doors—

CHORUS B.
New York's been overrun by whores!

Scene 3

Burlesque music. BETSY BOWEN bounds off her bed to begin an enticing dance. As she sings, HAMILTON emerges from behind the screen and puts on his shirt, leaving his pistol on the bed.

BOWEN (*singing*).
        I met the richest man in my life—
        He pleaded, Betsy, be my wife!

        Kind sir, said I, some girls do
        want to marry and be true—

        But when I hear my lover call,
        I'm not that sort of girl at all!

HAMILTON.
Betsy, I adore you, but my fortune's in danger.

BOWEN (*singing*).
        I won't fall for your song and dance—
        Don't want to fiddle with high finance!

HAMILTON.
My dear, I must distribute a letter
to friends who can discredit Burr.

BETSY BOWEN sits on the bed and picks up a quill to write.

BOWEN.
All right. We'll start.

HAMILTON. (*dictating his letter*).
Dear Sir:
Can it be true you support Colonel Burr
for president? Please reconsider.
I admit I despise Jefferson.
Yet good sense urges his election.
Aaron Burr is immoral, a voluptuary,
and bankrupt beyond redemption.

BOWEN *(interrupting)*.
Do you mean Burr must go begging?

HAMILTON *(aside to BOWEN)*.
That eel is too slippery to be caught
in debt. To satisfy his creditors,
he'll wed his daughter to a wealthy planter—
He's found her a young fop with money.

BOWEN.
Sell his dear daughter? Are you sure?

HAMILTON.
No one is *sure* about Burr... Please continue:

> *She resumes writing as he dictates the letter.*

Remember, the office cannot endure.
But do you believe Burr will abandon it?
Let us elect Jefferson; his mob will ruin
the prospect of a republic. Our own
General Hamilton then calls the army out—
No other citizen is fit to form
the monarchy this nation requires.
Meanwhile, Mr. Jefferson is our choice.
However, high office has its price:
He must promise half his appointments to us.
Burr will suspect nothing until he steps
into our snare, and we haul him up by the heel!

BOWEN.
If you swing Colonel Burr upside down
his privates will dangle—

HAMILTON.
You'll see that yet! Write this now:
... Make discreet us of this letter
among our friends. But reveal
my name to no one. I remain, your servant...

BOWEN.
How many copies will you want?

HAMILTON.
Make three before morning.

BOWEN.
Honey, this could be a busy night.

HAMILTON *(as they embrace).*
You tempt me terribly.

BOWEN.
And you are terrible to resist me.
Did you practice such restraint
when all our money was in your hands?

HAMILTON *(stiffly, as they step apart).*
I was Secretary of the Treasury.

BOWEN *(removing his glasses).*
We'll borrow this night in bed on our own account.
Invest it with interest, and when the sun arrives
to audit us with its hot suspicious eye,
you'll find your fortune is restored.

HAMILTON *(taking his coat and pistol).*
I don't dare bargain in bed with you
while Burr sleeps. Betsy,
write these letters. Every hour matters.

>   *They kiss. Putting on his glasses, HAMILTON exits.*

BOWEN *(singing).*
>   I won't fall for your song and dance—
>   Don't want to fiddle with high finance!

>   *A knock on the door. BURR opens it partway.*

BURR.
Darling, are you decent?

BOWEN.
I'm not naked, if that's what you mean.

>   *BURR enters. BOWEN climbs off the bed, they embrace.*

BURR *(looking around).*
Are you alone?

BOWEN.
Colonel, what a question!

BURR.
I know I'm not your first guest tonight.

BOWEN.
Not first, but not the least, either.

BURR.
Don't tease me; tell me you love Burr best.

BOWEN.
Is that so important?

BURR.
I won't stand in the shadow of anyone.

BOWEN.
Did you ever?

BURR.
I need to hear how dear I am to you.
The man in my looking-glass is a dark deceiver.

BOWEN *(turning, teasing).*
If I'm to be your mirror
you must cover my back with silver.

BURR *(circling to face her).*
But a woman *is* the mirror of my soul—
On your breast I'll be pale Narcissus,
I must see my image flower in your blue eyes.

BOWEN *(walking away).*
O, *damn* you! *Yes,* I desire you.

BURR.
Of all the men you know.

BOWEN.
My dear, Burr, that's not fair!

BURR.
Because a multitude may claim that honor.

BOWEN *(striding back to BURR)*.
You've brought to bed the boldest girls
in all New York. But when I wink
at another man I'm called a whore.

BURR.
I won't relent. I require it.

BOWEN *(routinely)*.
All right, dear.
No matter how many men admire me
it's you I adore.

    BURR is satisfied with the ritual. Now that it's over, both become cheerful. They kiss. Then BURR sees the sheets of paper on the table.

BURR.
That's my darling. . . Were you at work?

BOWEN.
Hamilton was here. You
followed him so near
he may have heard your horse.

BURR.
I sat my mare in a hickory grove
and watched him leave.

BOWEN *(as they caress)*.
Colonel, how clever you are.
He calls you an eel, too slick to be caught.

BURR.
I'm rising to my own bait.

    Stepping back, BURR seizes the letter.

Let me see his letter.

> *Burlesque music resumes softly while* BETSY BOWEN *removes* BURR'S *coat and pistols. Music stops.* BURR *reads silently.*

This is most bitter.
No man lives who has injured me more...
How many copies does he wish?

BOWEN *(holding up three fingers).*
Three.

BURR *(taking her hand, he opens a fourth finger).*
Add a fourth for me. My young men
will make these multiply
until they're in the hands of all our friends.

> *He kisses her palm and folds her fingers shut.*

BOWEN.
Everything he said of you is true.

BURR.
I'll spread his slander for him.
Let the public see Hamilton's treachery—
When Congress convenes, the majority will be mine.

> *Together they lie down on the bed.*

BOWEN.
What neat work you do with a few plain sheets.

> *Lights begin to dim.*

BURR. *(putting aside the letter).*
Not all sheets are for work.

BOWEN.
Is that a pointed remark?

BURR.
Pray that we make no copies now!

> *Laughter. Lights out. Enter* CHORUS A *to remove the screen as* BURR *and* BETSY BOWEN *exit behind it. Enter* CHORUS B *to roll the bed offstage.*

Scene 4

Lights come up as the WORKERS CHORUS brings two chairs to the small table. Enter JEFFERSON and DOLLEY MADISON to sit there, as the CHORUS divides, right and left.

CHORUS A.
Is it ambition? Is it pride?
Burr refuses to step aside.

CHORUS B.
Inauguration Day draws near—

JEFFERSON.
Why do we hear no word from Burr?

MADISON.
Have I turned into the town gossip?
Very well! Tom, he's been busy.
This month he married off his daughter
for a planter's fortune, to pay his debts.

JEFFERSON.
I hear the girl is so fond of her father
she's unfit for a lover.

MADISON.
I believe each letter from her fiancé
was written by Burr—

JEFFERSON *(rising, astonished).*
And copied over, in her lover's hand?

DOLLEY MADISON rises, reaches out to JEFFERSON. He takes her hands in his, drawing her near. While they talk, the CHORUS exits, returning with an early U.S. flag on a pole. They bring more chairs, a snare drum, and a triangle. They set a large Bible on the table.

MADISON.
The girl tells everyone the wit

in those pages charmed her heart. . .
But her hubby has only half his own.

JEFFERSON.
You know him?

MADISON.
The poor dolt danced at every ball this season.

JEFFERSON *(gleefully)*.
While Burr paid court to *her* on paper!

MADISON *(nods in agreement)*.
Her father was the voice of her suitor—
He's wooed and won his own daughter.

JEFFERSON *(releasing her, he steps back)*.
Tell me this tale about any man
but Aaron Burr, and I wouldn't believe it.
Did he dwell on the wedding, when you saw him?

MADISON.
The election alone occupied his mind.

JEFFERSON stretches, glances at the CHORUS at work.

JEFFERSON.
As it does mine.
It's late, let's adjourn.
Whoever wins this race, we'll know no peace.

DOLLEY MADISON exits. JEFFERSON stops in the doorway, watching the CHORUS carry a podium to center stage. The podium is wrapped in red, white, and blue bunting. They set it behind the small table, then wrap bunting around the table, for the Inaugural ceremony. Chairs are placed to right and left for spectators.

CHORUS *(while they work)*.
Have you heard the latest news?
Still our Congress can't choose!
They vote, they sleep, they rise to stalk
the snowy streets. They *talk*, and *talk*.

CHORUS A *(as HAMILTON enters)*.
Day and night, by tongue or pen,
Hamilton harangues these men—

HAMILTON.
Jefferson's a fool, but I forgive him
his mad philosophy. He has a heart.
Burr loves only Burr, you can bank on that!
Like Satan's serpent in the bower
the fiend has sold his soul for power!

CHORUS B *(as HAMILTON exits)*.
So he threatens, so he pleads,
until his strategy succeeds.

CHORUS A.
Now daybreak brings her messenger,
the Congressman from Delaware—

A man from CHORUS B approaches JEFFERSON; they whisper, then shake hands. He returns to his partner in the CHORUS.

CHORUS A *(watching the mime)*.
Jefferson is coy, but he listens.
Will the Virginian grant concessions?

CHORUS B.
A nod, a wink, a warm handshake,
mean more than words, make no mistake—

CHORUS.
One last vote... The tie is broken!
Now the majority has spoken...
President Jefferson!

Enter BURR and MARSHALL to join JEFFERSON at the podium. They are trailed by THEO, HAMILTON, BOWEN, and MADISON, who take seats as spectators.

CHORUS.
Inauguration Day! To both
Justice Marshall gives the oath.

Marching, the CHORUS *performs a well-meaning but unmusical "Yankee Doodle" with the snare drum and triangle, as the others join in, singing.* DOLLEY MADISON *dances with* JEFFERSON; HAMILTON *dances with* BETSY BOWEN. BURR *and* THEO *look on.*

ALL (*singing*).
"There sat Captain Washington
upon a slapping stallion,
giving orders to his men;
there must have been a million.

"Yankee Doodle, keep it up,
Yankee Doodle Dandy,
mind the music and the step,
and with the girls be handy!"

DOLLEY MADISON *urges* BURR *and* THEO *to dance. They refuse, but rise from their chairs.*

CHORUS.
Tonight there's joy, a jubilee!
The triumph of democracy!

CHORUS A.
But Burr seems somber. At his side
his daughter, who's a lonely bride,
declines to dance.

CHORUS B.
Abruptly they
bid their farewells, and steal away.

After BURR *and* THEO *exit, the festivity grows quiet.*

CHORUS.
This outcome has to bruise Burr's pride.
He almost stole the office for himself,
the greatest gamble of his life—
Or do you think he ever meant
only to be Vice President?
But this is not the night to doubt

our future. You know sure as hell
Jefferson will lead us well—
Everybody, dance and shout!

Curtain

ACT TWO

Scene 1

In the dim light upstage JEFFERSON watches BURR and MARSHALL, who stand downstage in full light. Just behind them are two chairs and the small table.

BURR (lifting the back of his red coat, toward JEFFERSON).
My one duty these days is to chair the Senate.
Chair! Yes, it's a labor that befits an ass!
John, to be Vice President is to sit
in the stocks. My talents languish,
I'm not included in the Cabinet—

MARSHALL (laughs at BURR'S gesture).
Colonel, count your blessings.
Jefferson's Cabinet is but a cupboard
where his pet mice hide, in that cold white house.

    He points his cane toward JEFFERSON, who remains motionless.

BURR (bitterly).
But *I'm* deprived of patronage for my friends.
Men must eat, and Burr's cupboard is bare.

MARSHAL (moves his cane like a broom handle).
Gossips in the Congress claim
he'll sweep you out, after this term.

BURR.
John, I can't turn my back on public life.
That black cloak of justice
suits your sober duty.
I'm more immodest—
I'll enter eternity wrapped in glory.

MARSHALL.
You'll find little opportunity in this city.

BURR.
Oh, absolutely. I ought to quit this place,
and the party too. It's out of my control.

But how do I walk away from my workers?
I survive on their support. And without
Burr, they have no stake in our society.
The blacks, the clerks who own no property.
The soldiers of the revolution. All forgotten.
Powerless, until they speak with one voice.

MARSHALL.
Bring them with you as far as they'll follow.

BURR.
First, I'll talk with Tom—

MARSHALL *(stabs the air with his cane).*
Careful not to turn your back.

    Exit MARSHALL. JEFFERSON approaches BURR. His costume is casual hereafter: slippers, an old robe over his shoulders. He has aged in office; his remarkable intelligence seems guarded, shrewd. Both men show their distrust.

BURR *(removing his coat).*
Mr. President, I'm at your service.

JEFFERSON *(hanging BURR'S coat on a chair).*
Aaron, you're often in my thoughts.

    Enter SALLY HEMINGS, a slim black woman, who serves tea, then withdraws to one side.

BURR.
But I'm not in your confidence.
I had hoped we'd meet more frequently.

HEMINGS *(a little defensively).*
We live quietly, as you see.

BURR *(to JEFFERSON).*
I thought you might value my judgment.

JEFFERSON *(archly).*
I treasure it.

BURR.
Too secretly, perhaps. People whisper
about bad blood between us.

JEFFERSON *(eyes BURR coolly)*.
I trust no tale that discredits you.

BURR *(heatedly)*.
You banish me from every sphere of power.
But I brought you here!
Is a life in exile my reward?
Vice President is the penalty for ambition?

JEFFERSON *(removes his slippers, rubs his feet)*.
I'm sorry, Aaron, that you're unhappy here.
It's so ill-suited for you, I assume
you won't want the office again.
The fact is, I do plan to replace you.

BURR.
Allow me to preserve my honor, and resign.
Appoint me to a lesser post—
I'll leave the capitol tonight.

HEMINGS *(to JEFFERSON)*.
What position could he have in mind?

BURR.
That huge Louisiana Territory
you purchased, sir.
It has no Governor.

JEFFERSON *(slides his feet into his slippers)*.
Colonel Burr, you know that territory
requires troops to defend the river.
To command so many men, others outrank you.

HEMINGS.
General Hamilton, for one.

BURR *(to JEFFERSON)*.
In my own home you told me,
"He's the evil genius of this country."

JEFFERSON.
All genius is of service.

BURR.
He's never held elective office.

JEFFERSON.
I know his limitations. However...
If *you* go west
you pass beyond my influence.

BURR.
As far as you wish.

JEFFERSON.
Too far to feel the cool shadow of the law.
With a frontier army under you command
at New Orleans—and your hand
on the neck of the Mississippi—No!

> *HEMINGS collects the tea service and exits.*

BURR.
You understand, I propose a proper bargain.
I'll put my young men to work
in your next campaign. You'll need New York—

JEFFERSON.
I won't have to bargain for re-election.

BURR.
I envy you that luxury.

JEFFERSON.
You're at leisure to pursue other pleasures.

BURR *(shrugs).*
Each morning I take target practice.
My pistols are my only exercise.

> *He looks about for SALLY HEMINGS, as she returns.*

Or did you mean a more sociable sport?

JEFFERSON.
I thought by now you'd have married again, Aaron.

BURR *(putting on his coat).*
Is that why you give me no duties?
The second citizen in the land, and I'm left unemployed,
so I might find a bride.
If a wife is such a virtue
perhaps you'll want one, too.

> *Lights dim upstage on JEFFERSON and HEMINGS, who watch BURR meet MARSHALL downstage, in full light.*

MARSHALL.
You see, you have no hopes here.

BURR.
John, I'm coming home. Go tell New York
Burr will run for Governor.

> *MARSHALL embraces BURR; they step apart.*

MARSHALL.
Remember, you serve neither party now.
You must walk a fine wire above both.

> *BURR, arms outstretched, places one foot before the other, as he mimics a high-wire walker, glancing down at the imagined crowd below him.*

BURR.
I'll keep my balance. And balance my accounts.
John, I haven't paid for my last election. . .
If I fall now, I must sell my home at auction.

> *BURR pretends to leap from the wire and land safely, as JEFFERSON and HEMINGS watch him. Then they exit.*

MARSHALL.
You'll live to laugh at these troubles. The voters
won't hear out Hamilton again,

he's half mad now. But beware:
you threaten his hold on their hearts.

BURR.
Whoever owns their hearts, I'll win their votes.

Scene 2

The WORKERS CHORUS *speaks to the audience while* BURR, *at his desk, reads a newspaper.*

CHORUS A.
No report has brought more cheer to Burr
than his daughter's news—she has a son!

CHORUS B.
She named the boy Aaron, for her father.
Which lightens his heart in the gloom of defeat.

BURR *(to* CHORUS*).*
This gloom you speak of isn't all
my doing. That bastard Hamilton
becomes my shadow. Everywhere I go
his dark influence follows me.

CHORUS A *(to audience).*
You saw him leave the capitol in haste
to run for Governor of New York,
but Burr lost that race before he arrived.

CHORUS B.
All those scandals Hamilton reported—
His handbills blossomed overnight
on every unwashed wall within New York.

BURR *(slapping the table with the newspaper).*
Every snap of his jaws cripples my career.

CHORUS A *(taking* BURR'S *paper).*
And the cur lopes home unharmed
although you're a sure shot.

CHORUS B *(reading the paper).*
Hamilton told two hundred at a tavern:
Colonel Burr inspires rebellion.

BURR.
As all men do, who admit their desires.

CHORUS A *(waving the paper).*
There's more...
He gives his opinion of your character.

BURR.
How many times must I taste his venom?

CHORUS B.
He says you sold your daughter—

BURR *(nodding).*
To that Souther planter—

CHORUS A.
To pay your debts.

BURR.
Then why am I bankrupt today? No, no,
that's cold porridge. He knows
that old tale won't warm over.
He must offer his hated public
some hot delicacy to tempt their tongue.

CHORUS B.
Well, sir, that's what he's done.

CHORUS *(as BURR looks with interest).*
General Hamilton has begun the rumor
that you're the father of Aaron, Junior.

BURR *(long pause).*
Theo's baby?
By her own papa?
He'll have to answer *this*.

> BURR *whirls and draws one pistol, taking aim at an imaginary target.*

CHORUS A.
Can he hide from the echo of his own words?

CHORUS B.
Only the walls of a tomb will stop gossip.

>*Returning the pistol to his belt, BURR leads the CHORUS toward the doorway.*

BURR.
He'll tell no more tales about Burr.
I'll silence him for all time—
Haul him from his bed and drag him here!

>*CHORUS exits. BURR returns to his desk. The left side of the stage is dim as THEO enters there. When she is seen in a cone of light, she's oblivious to the dim room, as if present only in spirit. BURR takes up the globe.*

BURR.
What a wonder is this sphere
hung in heaven like a star—
Still more lovely when we see
every delight in its design
within our grasp. So might men
hope to cultivate its bloom,
watered, pretty, plentiful.
O, to hold the whole glad globe
in my hand!
 But this bright rind
conceals bitter fruit. Under
its skin is damp dirt, the dismal
home of worms. Like all men I
dream I'm immortal. Until the hour
of my last deed in darkness
when I dine on this dish alone,
and the taste of time stains my mouth.

>*BURR puts down the globe. THEO replies as if he'd spoken directly to her.*

THEO.
Talk of death discredits you.
A man who leaps with life—

BURR.
Missy, I must not avoid the word.
Since the night your mother died,
I'm mindful of it every minute.

THEO.
No! Some nuisance turns you to it.

BURR (*his mood a little lighter*).
I'll write a letter to my daughter...

>   *BURR takes out the locket, kisses it, and returns it to his pocket.*

My dear Theo,
Ignore all those horrid reports
of your Papa's behavior. Enemies distort
my passion for political intrigue.
And such bizarre rumors from the boudoir!
If *half* their fantasies were true
would I have strength enough to write to you?

>   *BURR laughs at his own joke. THEO holds a letter; she looks up from reading it, and laughs. BURR continues.*

But how sad when our future seems uncertain—
You and I must climb in the blaze of noon,
never creep down the fence like a listless vine.

THEO.
Papa always has an alarming plan.

BURR.
I send a copy of my will tonight. Don't ask why.
With those who are disappointed by my gifts,
I heartily agree. I leave everyone so little,
because I have so little left... They may admire
the form, if not the substance, of that remark.

THEO.
You give me more than life itself, Father.
Death were better, than not to be your daughter.

BURR.
As for amorous affairs, I slept once
with a woman as flat as a fence.
Strait was the gate and narrow was the way!
Another wench was well-endowed, alas,
not in a lucrative trust. I should say
she was well-reared. A virtue only in a horse!

THEO.
You tease me, to throw me off the trace.

BURR.
The best behaved have bored me, I forget the rest.
The thought of marriage is like alchemy—
Today I'm weak as water, tomorrow stiff as a stick!
Churlish girl, you give me no counsel.
"Go hang yourself, if you please," says my pet.
"Or don't dare do it, and live long yet."

THEO.
You never needed my permission, Papa.
If you haven't made a proposal
it's because your mind wanders. Or your *eye*.

BURR.
Missy, my romantic efforts have limits.
Don't forget, I'm a grandfather. As to that,
tell me about young Aaron: is the lad alive?
I believe you would have written, if he died.

THEO.
I write to you every week.

BURR.
Darling, don't mistake your father's chiding—
You alone have made my heart happy.
From you I learn true grace and beauty.
Now, you must prepare your son, as well...
Show all the world the merit of your soul!
Missy, my fate has flown from my hands—
If I should never write to you again,

I pray you will remember that I send
on this plain paper all my love to you.
—Chère amie, adieu

Lights dim quickly on BURR. *Light gradually dims on* THEO, *down to darkness. She exits. As the lights come up, the* CHORUS *enters with* HAMILTON.

HAMILTON.
Your mob tells me we must meet,
though it's the dead of night.
What's your reason?

BURR.
Reason be damned, sir.
I'm sensitive to your vile remarks.

HAMILTON.
You're too tender. . . What words pricked you?

BURR (*showing him the newspaper*).
A certain rumor shames my daughter.
It invites immoral speculation.

HAMILTON.
Only to your wicked imagination.

BURR.
I require satisfaction.
An honest duel should settle our dispute.

HAMILTON.
I can't account for every word I've uttered
in twenty years of public life.

BURR (*waving the paper*).
This account must be paid.

HAMILTON.
At an awful price!
I never was your equal with a pistol.

BURR *(with an exaggerated bow)*.
I shall prove that point on the field of honor.

CHORUS *(as BURR moves toward his desk)*.
Words fail to answer, in the teeth of anger.
Each man must hear his pistol speak.

CHORUS A *(to HAMILTON)*.
Heads are hot, it's the summer sun.
Let the Colonel cool down.

CHORUS B *(in disagreement)*.
This scheme has grown too grave,
Burr won't withdraw his challenge.

CHORUS A *(to HAMILTON)*.
Default then, damn it. Don't be foolish—
What can a duel accomplish?
When all's said and done,
it's pistols for two, coffee for one!

    BURR *signals the* CHORUS *to remove his desk and chair, and he follows them offstage.*

HAMILTON.
I can never command your army,
never direct my party,
unless I oppose him with his own weapon.

CHORUS B.
And lodge a lead ball in his heart?

HAMILTON.
I will not.

CHORUS B.
Not to defend yourself is suicide.

HAMILTON *(as CHORUS A returns)*.
I won't shoot Burr.
I'll fire high in the air,
so the Colonel might reconsider.

CHORUS.
Then you'd better settle your debts.
Write your will tonight,
General, you're bout to leave
your white-haired years to the grave.

HAMILTON.
Lord know, I'm ready. I've lived too long
in this damned democracy. Who can teach you
unity? You'll follow any flag—
You people are a beast who must be led
to your destiny by a demagogue.
This country cries out for a king.
The title terrifies you, yet
you're Britain's bastard children, begging
Papa to pay your bills, put food on your table.

CHORUS.
No one here would *dare* to wear a crown!
And folks will miss your point, after all.
They'll say you were struck down by a devil.

HAMILTON *(moving toward the door)*.
Then my death will darken his career
for all time. The hour I fall
I'll bury Burr in hell. Hereafter,
he's an assassin in the nation's soul.
People will pay homage to me,
perpetually. Do you understand?
Whether you do or not, here's my last thought—
As a Christian man the choice was never mine.
If Lucifer invites me to a duel,
I'm not free to decline.

    HAMILTON *exits. The* CHORUS *remains for a moment, their heads in their hands. Then they remove the chairs and return to the bare stage.*

CHORUS.
We'll meet once more, across the Hudson River
grey as gun-metal in the glow of dawn.
At Weehawken we'll draw our boats ashore. . .

BURR enters, bringing an umbrella and a black box which he hands to the CHORUS.

... where rock and brush protect the drowsy spot
from public view. *Hush.* Listen. Our fate
is a web of whispers, ripped by pistol shot,
which wakens all our countrymen, too late!

Scene 3

The duelists salute. CHORUS A and B serve as their seconds, stepping off ten paces for them. BURR takes the locket from his vest, while HAMILTON wipes his glasses and puts them on. Both watch as the CHORUS removes two large pistols from the black box, bringing one to BURR, downstage right, and the other to HAMILTON, who is upstage center. HAMILTON removes his glasses, then shades his eyes with his hand.

BURR.
What's the difficulty?

CHORUS A.
The sun, sir. It's just over the trees.

BURR.
I gave him his choice of sides.
Why did he want to face the sun?

CHORUS B.
Your guess is as good as ours.

BURR.
Shall we get on?

CHORUS.
Gentlemen:
When you hear the word *'pre-sent'*
then you may fire, as you wish.
Are you ready?

BURR.
We are.

HAMILTON.
Ready.

CHORUS *(after a long pause).*
Preeee–sent!

    BURR *and* HAMILTON *take aim. When* BURR *fires,* HAMILTON'S *arm rises, his pistol fires, he falls.* BURR *looks back overhead, on the line of the shot.* CHORUS B *kneels over* HAMILTON, *their heads bowed as if listening to him.*

BURR.
Why so pale? Is he dead?

CHORUS A.
Not yet.

BURR.
Our gunfire stunned my ear. Did you hear him?

CHORUS B.
He whispered, "This is a mortal wound."

BURR.
Do you think so?

CHORUS B.
That's all he said.
That voice in man which calls to God
left his throat.

BURR *(retrieving the glasses).*
He won't need these glasses again. Poor fool.
He could never see the folly of baiting me.
Now his name owes its fame to mine.

CHORUS A *(handing him the umbrella).*
Go, before another soul sees you.

BURR.
Yes; I don't want more witnesses to this.

    BURR *exits, crouching behind the open umbrella. The* CHORUS *carries* HAMILTON *offstage. They return bringing what appears to be a stone monument, a grey obelisk which they set down to mark the spot where* HAMILTON *had fallen.*

CHORUS *(to the audience while placing the marker).*
You people knew this had to happen.
You heard how Hamilton spread
that dirt about Burr and his daughter.

CHORUS B.
Never mind a little soap and water,
a smear like that won't wash away.
Some words cast their shadow across your life—

CHORUS B.
Their darkness follows you. Day after day
it crawls through the grass. Weary
at last, you lie down in your grave.
Still that slander stains your bones.

CHORUS A.
But then, as if its author slew himself,
once his wicked thought has left his mouth,
his blood begins to spill, it darkens the soil.

CHORUS B.
Hamilton had such princely pride
he'd never bow to Burr. Not
even in death. A willing victim,
he hopes to bury Burr beneath him.

CHORUS A *(to audience).*
But do you think his death was suicide?

CHORUS B.
Well, it's a sorry story, and his wife
won't be the only beauty wild with grief.

CHORUS A *(they nod in agreement).*
God knows! We'll wager more than one
wench will toss all night in sorrow—

CHORUS B.
And toss in bed with Burr tomorrow.

CHORUS *(stepping back from the monument).*
Look, life's a gamble: the odds favor

no one who sits at the table—
Does anybody quit while he's ahead?

    The CHORUS moves downstage, still divided.

Now Hamilton, who would be king, is dead.
Among our nation's martyrs, here he lies.
While Burr, who won't pretend to piety,
but dealt *our* hand in this society,
flees like a murderer before our eyes.

                   Curtain

ACT THREE

Scene 1

The WORKERS CHORUS carries onto the bare stage a small table and two chairs.

CHORUS.
Still the stunned nation grieves.
We take the street, return to work—

CHORUS A.
Burr is indicted in New York—

CHORUS B.
Opponents hope to hang him—

CHORUS.
What can he do but flee?

    BURR enters, bringing a blanket roll to the table.

Like many men he wanders toward the west,
a land of unmapped opportunity.

CHORUS A.
He'll possess the Mississippi at its Gulf,
and the gold of Mexico—

CHORUS B.
            Or reign
over a realm of dream and ruin,
all that's left him in this life.

    BURR opens the blanket, revealing four rifles.

But glory beckons as never before,
and Burr will be its Emperor.

BURR *(handing each man a rifle).*
We're about to undertake a task
Hamilton wouldn't dare to dream.

CHORUS.
Let's not defile the dead. He never loved
the likes of us, that's true. Do you?

BURR *(steps back to appraise them)*.
Enough to offer food and drink,
and all the land that you can farm.

CHORUS.
When do we collect?

BURR.
You've come this far. Keep faith, dear friends,
we'll carve up half a continent. And I
mean no harm to Hamilton; that sad man
lives in history now. As for Jefferson
and his democracy, the passion
for power is a flame that will consume
all matter the mind invents.
It leaps the walls of my heart. Escapes
into thin air, where ideas tremble
like dry leaves. A spark, and *puuf!*
they frizzle in a blaze. All die out.
The fine ashes of philosophy
float to earth, cool, pale—
A brief snowfall that melts underfoot.

    BURR *stamps his boots; then he approaches the* CHORUS, *clapping their shoulders, enlisting their support.*

I must act on my own behalf—
I leave behind my countrymen who plan
to kill me. Arms and a thousand men
like you surround me on this island,
sufficient forces for our insurrection.

CHORUS *(with military bearing)*.
We'll seize New Orleans, then launch our assault
on Mexico.

CHORUS A.
We'll march away a million souls to work
our land—

CHORUS B.
Float home a gold fortune for your vault.

BURR.
I'll pay every soldier in full measure.
Today you serve, tomorrow you're a squire!

    The CHORUS exits with eager spirit, as THEO and WILLIAM LOVE enter. BURR and THEO sit at the table.

Well, well, it's William Love. Any mail?

LOVE *(angry)*.
I'm afraid not, Colonel.

BURR.
True love fears nothing. Or is it true,
love fears nothing? Love appears
pale with worry, fraught with doubt.
Love lies limp all night, and now creeps out
like a quiet cloud across our path.

THEO.
Did you say love lies?

BURR.
Never! *Our* love is ever true.

LOVE.
It's clear that we dislike each other,
but I'm not employed at your pleasure.
I'm the servant of your host, Mr. Blennerhassett.

BURR *(turning to THEO)*.
Love cannot serve two masters, Missy.

THEO.
Oh, but he's such a love.
Papa, take pity, you tease him too much.

BURR.
Only to amuse us both, and mask my despair.

THEO.
Still no news from Wilkinson? You *must* start soon.

BURR.
I await his word to launch our attack.
Every day's delay endangers us.
He did swear to surrender New Orleans
when I arrive. Our army now stands ready
to raft down river. Does the fat cow balk?
Fear for its hide has turned its blood to milk.

THEO.
No! At this late date he doesn't dare
betray you, Papa. You bought him fair and square.

BURR.
I trust him the length of this little island.

LOVE.
Down by the pier, sir, where your barges strain
under their burden, I tally two hundred
kegs of gunpowder. How do you explain—

THEO *(claps her hands with glee)*.
We'll light the starry heaven! Jefferson
might view our fireworks from his hilly farm.

BURR *(putting on eyeglasses)*.
Hush now...Here's our host.

THEO.
You'll be Blennerhassett?

BURR *(to LOVE)*.
Forgive me if I mimic Mr. Blennerhassett.
These glasses, I might mention,
are a legacy from General Hamilton.
Like your employer, he saw all things darkly.

THEO.
Well, we'll play! Let's begin.
Tell me, Blenny,
why won't Wilkinson reply to Papa?

BURR.
That gross gut has no stomach for adventure.
Too much fat hides his heart.

THEO.
Why, you've caught his scent, sir.
Your nose sees better than your eyes.
When Burr is Emperor
you'll be our chief counsellor.

LOVE *(indignant)*.
He'll earn any honors he receives.

THEO.
He gives us lodging for our troops.
Money for munitions.
He'll have the distinction he deserves.

    LOVE bows and exits.. BURR gropes toward THEO, who laughs.

Poor Blenny *is* blind to our purpose.

BURR *(removing his glasses)*.
He can't even find his way to his wife.
Tell me, was Maggie ill this morning.?

THEO *(her hands on her stomach)*.
She's worried sick over a weighty manner.

BURR.
It's a ticklish situation.

THEO *(firmly)*.
Papa, the lady is a *little* pregnant.
Deny that you're her lover.

BURR *(smiling)*.
What ungrateful guest would refuse
the wife of his host?
If my good manners make me the father
of her child, I'm flattered by the honor.

THEO.
How gallant you are. And guilty, too?

BURR.
Missy, I've made some study of theology.
From old Jonathan Edwards to this day
there's a history of that illness in our family...
But our faults are only the absence of God's graces.
And your Papa is ever gracious.

THEO.
To a fault, I fear.

BURR *(impatient).*
I'm too rational for religion.

THEO *(shakes her head).*
Papa, you're too proud to worship.

BURR.
Dear, we wouldn't be *here* if I were humble.

> *THEO laughs. BURR poses her, then he stands behind her.*

Now we must review our recruits.
Theo, there. Papa stands here.

> *The CHORUS enters, carrying their rifles. They march eagerly, and salute at random.*

THEO *(laughing).*
Look at their salutes!...
I wonder, when we conquer Mexico,
will these troops parade us in triumph?

> *The CHORUS lifts THEO, and they carry her around on their shoulders.*

BURR.
You'll ride through every village on a throne.

THEO *(looking up).*
With a roof of red feathers for shade?

BURR.
Are you already spoiled?
I only hope Maggie might deliver—

CHORUS *(as they set THEO down).*
Before we'll need a regiment to lift her.

> *Laughter. They salute, and resume marching.*

THEO.
How did you gain so many recruits?

BURR.
I promised one hundred acres to every man.

THEO.
So these are soldiers of fortune?

BURR.
I pray they are. I wrote to Wilkinson,
"The gods invite us to glory!"
These men will make *our* fortune soon.

THEO.
Then we can pay Blenny for our expenses.

BURR *(as the CHORUS stops and listens).*
Lord knows, I'm destitute. I can't afford
to meet my creditors in a dark street.
But this exploit will earn us Aztec gold.
We'll join our fleet with chain, from hull to hull—
A blockade across the Mississippi.
Every barge a powder keg. Troops on guard.
I'll charge tariff on all river traffic.

THEO.
Papa, what a wicked thought!
You'll take a tremendous revenue
from furs, and meal. Sugar. Salt.

BURR.
Ample amounts to settle my debts.
And one pleasure beyond price: the power
to instruct by my example. Let Jefferson
dream his community, Burr knows better.
The soul is solitary. We're never free
when we chant in chorus with society.

He lowers his voice, his hand on his heart.
Listen to that little voice beneath your breast,
Missy, it speaks to you alone.
No one else is *here* to hear.
Yet every appetite dwells within,
like a nun devoted to a single passion.

    He reaches out to Theo, who gives him her hands.

Think of my love for you, my only bliss.

    He releases her.

Soon the world will see my pride in you
and your son, when we three occupy our throne.

THEO *(putting an arm around her father).*
Papa, can you forget the President
commands the army?

BURR *(with a wave of his hand).*
As rain commands the wind that blows it on.
Whisper the world "rebellion" in their ears
and Tom's troops will be ours.

THEO.
And our young men, in their green years?

BURR *(as the CHORUS begins to march once more).*
The best that bloom on earth!
These are the flower of manhood among us
and they won't wither until their death.

THEO.
I stand downwind of them—
Their fragrance is not a sober scent.

BURR.
Let the lads go cross-eyed drunk on claret
or corn liquor. Let them be whiskey-dizzy.
They'll slaughter a sober President. He'd rather
bed his black beauty than fight this war
against Burr. But their drill's done. Dismiss them.

THEO *(steps forward, her hands on her hips).*
Halt!. . . Fall out!

    CHORUS A *sits.* CHORUS B *straggles offstage, returning with a snare drum and a triangle.*

BURR.
I must leave, Missy. When all's ready
I'll write for you to join me.

THEO.
It grows dark.
Won't you wait for daybreak?

BURR *(his hand makes a rippling motion).*
Night will float me under every eye
watching the water. At dawn
I'll draw into shore, to hide until dusk.

THEO.
I wish I were tucked in your luggage trunk.

BURR.
Wish no further.
You are baggage indeed
if you don't obey your father.

THEO.
Oh, I shall.

BURR.
Because you must stay, you go
with me night and day,
daughter of my soul.

    BURR *and* THEO *exit. To the tune of "Yankee Doodle," the* CHORUS *clowns downstage, as* JEFFERSON *enters with* SALLY HEMINGS *and* JOHN MARSHALL *at the start of the song.*

Scene 2

CHORUS A *(singing).*
"To ease the weight of state affairs
I like to sport and dally,
then rest my head with all its cares
in the shady lap of Sally."

CHORUS B *(singing).*
"Yankee Doodle loves to cuddle
with a wench so handy.
To breed a flock of slaves, you see,
a black gal is just dandy."

The CHORUS *shoulders arms and marches off, laughing.* JEFFERSON *and MARSHALL sit by the table, while* HEMINGS *waits in the doorway.*

JEFFERSON.
Sally, sit with us,. You warm my heart.

HEMINGS.
In this chill weather
you want to keep your friends close
like live coals.

JEFFERSON.
They're too bleak, beside you.
even a judge in his black robe
might pale
when he hears Burr's plot.

JEFFERSON leads her over, kisses her neck. MARSHALL *rises and* HEMINGS *takes his seat.* JEFFERSON *sits, unfolding a letter.*

Justice Marshall is about to trace the evil map of Burr's mind.

MARSHALL.
I've read letters about Burr before.

JEFFERSON.
Here's one in code from his own hand,
deciphered by a false friend—

General Wilkinson, who shared his scheme
to seize New Orleans. Burr writes to his recruits:
> "I, Aaron Burr, begin my enterprise.
> My troops rendezvous on the Ohio River,
> while at New Orleans the English navy
> waits to welcome us. Eager sailors
> from our gulf fleet will join with theirs."

JEFFERSON looks at MARSHALL, then continues reading.

> "I give all orders to my followers;
> Wilkinson shall lead my officers.
> Downriver I'll sail my army,
> a thousand soldiers in swift boats
> to surprise the city.
>   I guarantee
> this endeavor with my life and honor,
> and with the best blood of our country.
> The gods invite us to glory..."

MARSHALL.
Burr wrote that?

JEFFERSON.
Do you doubt it? For a minute?
He's desperate, without his workers' support.
In politics one man is none.
John, how could you encourage him?

MARSHALL.
When you gave him no role in your government
his fortune fell.
Yet Aaron Burr is a man of worth—

JEFFERSON.
John, will you hear the truth?
Burr doesn't own a dollar, and he'll never
earn another. Forget his pearl pistols,
his velvet coat, those high-tone boots.
His pocket is as empty as his heart.
The best blood of this country is not
in the veins of men who stack up guns
for their private grudges. Drill

by firelight and plot to rule
a land of dreams. Our best blood flows
from a community of individuals who share
their minds and hands; their craft and thought.
This is the truly human union.

MARSHALL.
People argue that you ask each one
to sacrifice too much for his fellow man.
If all grow weak the yoke weighs more.
And when was wisdom a matter of the majority?

JEFFERSON (*curtly*).
Or won by treachery?

MARSHALL.
Burr's belligerent language is proof only
of his ambition. That letter
lacks the smell of powder.
I won't lock him up for a lawless thought.

JEFFERSON (*shaking the letter*).
Here's his plot—

MARSHALL.
Remember, the republic too is an idea.
Not one of Nature's laws. It exists
first in our minds and hearts. However,
Burr and his troops have fled beyond its border.

JEFFERSON (*looking again at the letter*).
I pity those young men that he's misled.
He'll never march them into Mexico.
His ambition is to overthrow our army
and drown his President in the Potomac.
But I'll be bone dry while Burr is strung
in the wind. I have the evidence in hand.

MARSHALL.
That letter indicts Wilkinson as well.
And he's *your* General.

JEFFERSON *(as he pockets the letter)*.
John, I'll pardon General Wilkinson,
or anyone caught in our snare
who testifies against Burr.
What court tries this case?

MARSHALL.
Richmond, Virginia.

JEFFERSON *(alarmed)*.
In your jurisdiction!
Where you oppose your President
with the ill will of a jealous politician.

MARSHALL.
I won't vacate the bench because of your bias.
Even Burr deserves an impartial trial.

JEFFERSON *(rising)*.
Judges will run this nation into ruin!
Burr is a traitor—

MARSHALL.
His words are not an act of war.

JEFFERSON.
I can't endure the luxury of your long robes.
How often they hide a villain
while his victim cries for aid!

MARSHALL *(cautioning)*.
But here's a question to consider—
Burr was always a brash lawyer.
Suppose he sways Virginia to his cause?

JEFFERSON *(circling behind HEMINGS)*.
Throw him in jail until his trial.

MARSHALL.
I won't allow it.

JEFFERSON *(stares at MARSHALL)*.
After his fall, did Satan go free on bail?

MARSHALL.
The devil knew he'd lost his soul.

JEFFERSON *(his hand on HEMINGS' shoulder)*.
But your damned Burr doesn't know the difference!
Not one sentiment softens his heart.
While he bribes his troops with bankrupt hopes,
your friend persuades a general to surrender
the city I sent him to guard.
It's the talent of a tyrant, and his art
appalls us all. Should he prevail,
he'll plunder the republic for his own profit.
That's why he's in it. You'll see
the canvas of our country smeared
by the hand of unrelenting greed.

MARSHALL *(thoughtful)*.
Once he gains New Orleans—

JEFFERSON *(stroking HEMINGS' neck)*.
He'll choke off traffic on the Mississippi.
All the West lies at his mercy.
He'll own an empire overnight
whether he invades Mexico or not.

MARSHALL.
You'll order his arrest?

JEFFERSON *(nodding)*.
Tonight I'll write the proclamation,
and alert every citizen.

MARSHALL *(as he exits)*.
I'll leave you to your thoughts.

JEFFERSON *(softly)*.
Burr's neck is in the noose—
But he must hang in the sun and rain
long enough to rot the rope.
When he's overripe, he'll drop like a stone.

HEMINGS.
This sight will chill the heart—

JEFFERSON *(taking her hand)*.
Treason is a cold-blooded crime.

    HEMINGS rises. JEFFERSON steps toward the door but stops, her hand still in his, as if she holds him to the spot.

HEMINGS.
But you must catch him at it.

JEFFERSON.
Let him slip downstream unaware. We'll fish him out—

HEMINGS.
Show him to the public then at large—

JEFFERSON *(gives HEMINGS his arm)*.
Still glimmering with guile. To be tried
for high treason, and guilty of the charge.

    Arm in arm, JEFFERSON and HEMINGS watch the CHORUS replace the small table with the larger one, left, where the lights dim to darkness as the CHORUS now sits drinking. JEFFERSON and HEMINGS exit.

Scene 3

BURR enters with his blanket roll. Kneeling, he tries to light a fire with flint and twigs. THEO enters, shivering.

THEO.
Colonel Burr? Is that you?

BURR.
That voice! My child!

THEO *(rushing to BURR).*
Papa! Papa!
We saw your mooring from the river
and we rowed over.

BURR.
Whatever you saw it wasn't mine
unless you were drowned among the damned
catfish. I sunk my boat to the bottom.
Some lost soul is wandering in these woods—
Where are the others?

THEO.
They won't follow.
Militia men have overrun the island.
They ransacked Blenny's house and took your guns.

BURR.
But you and the boy slipped free?

THEO.
One of Blenny's blacks will guide us to Kentucky,
where we'll hide. First I had to find you...

BURR *(putting his coat across her shoulders).*
That black man saved the boy's life. And yours.
But we're near Natchez now—better leave
before he's taken for a slave.
I'll go alone to New Orleans
where Wilkinson will deliver the city.

THEO *(kisses him).*
Until then, Papa.

> *THEO exits. BURR tries again to start a fire, then he kicks the twigs in disgust, as LAWYER PERKINS enters with a lantern, not yet seen by BURR.*

BURR.
This wood's too wet.

PERKINS.
God alone can strike fire in a storm.
Lightnin' like tonight...
None of us has the knack.

BURR *(turning, he draws his pistol).*
What brings you here?

PERKINS.
That skiff moored over there.

> *BURR aims the pistol between PERKINS' eyes, as if he might shoot the man for being a fool.*

BURR.
From this mud of the Mississippi our mad God
makes a half-wit. *Bless* my luck!
I've half a mind to toss him back—

> *BURR returns the pistol to his belt.*

I hardly thought you came on foot.
I meant: What's your business?

PERKINS
A proclamation from our President.

> *From his cloak he takes a newspaper, setting it down beside the lantern. He kneels, reading:*

> "A warning to every citizen—
> Certain people now plot a military expedition.
> You must keep clear of them.
> Officers of the law, be vigilant
> and bring to punishment
> anyone engaged in this conspiracy."

BURR.
He'll punish all persons who are engaged?
Why, let them marry. In time
their punishment will fit their crime.

PERKINS.
This is no jest.

BURR.
Indeed it's not. That notice is a net
flung over the country to catch his adversary.

PERKINS.
I hear it's Colonel Burr.

BURR.
What's his crime?

PERKINS *(rising)*.
High treason, so they say.

BURR.
High treason! Why?

PERKINS.
After the traitors have their day in court
we'll hang them high.

BURR.
Hang them?

PERKINS.
On trees.

BURR *(wincing; sarcastic)*.
Were you ever a scholar?

PERKINS *(shakes his head)*.
Name is Lawyer Perkins. Thought I don't know books,
no more than the muddle of this woods.
But I'm told I'll find a tavern near.

> BURR *opens his blanket, wraps it over his shoulders.*

BURR.
A roof and dry bedding would be a blessing.

PERKINS.
A jar of rum won't hurt me none.
That river kept my skiff pitchin' so,
I don't feel natural onshore, standin' straight.

BURR.
I see you've practiced at the bar.
No man has argued better for his rum.
Lawyer, bring your light.

PERKINS (*lifting his lantern*).
I have it. Come.

Darkness on the right half of the stage, as light comes up on the table at the left. The CHORUS sits drinking. PERKINS is offered a cup and he takes it, then he spreads out his paper on the table. BURR, with the blanket on his shoulders, waits at the edge of the light. PERKINS begins to read from the paper as he drinks:

Says here: "Certain people now plot a military expedition..."

CHORUS A.
Who the hell are you?

PERKINS (*looking up*).
An agent of your President.
We're sent to warn all citizens—

CHORUS B.
—That you're coming?

PERKINS (*over BURR'S laughter*).
Why, no, I'm here to tell you of a scheme
to take Texas and New Orleans
and march into Mexico—

CHORUS A.
That rumor had longer legs than yours.

CHORUS B.
It ran through here weeks ago.

PERKINS.
Well, a militia has caught them in the act.
Found an army of riflemen, trainin' to attack.
And flatboats weighted low in the water—
barges ablaze with weapons. Though not no more.
And the chief conspirator is Aaron Burr.

BURR.
Who was nowhere near?

PERKINS.
His name darkens all the papers, sir.
Ink as black as Burr's blood. Listen here:

> "TWO THOUSAND DOLLARS REWARD
> FOR THE ARREST OF COLONEL AARON BURR
> FORMER VICE PRESIDENT
> OF THESE UNITED STATES"

BURR.
Two thousand dollars, sir?
Is any man worth more?

PERKINS.
That money, and mention of his letter,
ought to trap a badger like Burr.

BURR.
What letter?

PERKINS *(handing the paper to him)*.
This one he wrote to Wilkinson.

BURR *(reading)*.
"I, Aaron Burr, begin my enterprise.
My troops rendezvous on the Ohio River..."

> *BURR thrusts aside the newspaper.*

I enlisted to serve with Wilkinson
when I heard talk of this trouble.
If I might borrow a horse from one of you
I'll ride tonight to join the General's troops.

PERKINS.
You may be one of his recruits
but you wear the boots of a gentlemen.

> PERKINS *flings back* BURR'S *blanket and pulls the pistols from his belt. He circles Burr, guns ready.*

BURR.
This fool is blind drunk.

PERKINS.
Sober enough to see that pointed toe,
the high shine of your heel.
Hardly fit for hikin' in the woods.

> BURR *leaps onto the table and raises his arms.*

BURR.
Of course I'm Colonel Burr, you ass!

> *He turns to the* CHORUS.

I'm an officer from the Army
of the Revolution. I demand
to meet your civil authority.

PERKINS.
Why, that's me—
even a country lawyer is an officer of the court.
I'll do more than meet you, sir,
I'll take you into custody myself.
Outside, and we'll saddle you a horse.

BURR (*as the* CHORUS *pulls him from the table*).
In that rain?

PERKINS.
Rain won't hurt us none.
I'll wipe my hands dry
on two thousand dollars, thanks to you.

BURR (*reaching out to the* CHORUS).
Good men, you must defend me. You labor
a lifetime for one opportunity

to decide your destiny—
You're the conscience of this country.
Release me! You know me...
You know I honor the dignity
of every man or woman
opposed to authority.
I support your desire to excel
beyond the walls of a school or meeting-hall...

CHORUS.
Destiny, honor, dignity...
Big words tell little lies.
You murdered a man as desperate as yourself
and twice as wise.

BURR.
Murder? Never! I did kill Hamilton
in that damned duel—

CHORUS.
Now you aim at Jefferson.

BURR.
The sooner slain the better.
Because he believes his soul
is the equal of every other,
he can't admit superiority
when it spits in his face!
We're condemned to the rule
of a common majority.
In time this government will claim
we owe our liberty and our labor
for the right to be no better than our brother.
But I tell you truly...

    BURR catches himself wandering; he pulls up abruptly. His look now is critical, as if he's reviewing his troops.

The best blood of the country, I called you once,
when you were in rebellious bloom and proud
to show the world the color of your courage.
Look at you! The sight hurts my heart.

Tonight you wait to be ordered about
like weeds bent low in the wind—
the harvest of this damned democracy.

PERKINS.
Save the speech until we meet in court,
Colonel Burr. I'll deliver you
dead or alive, it makes no difference to me.

> *Putting the pistols in his own belt, LAWYER PERKINS slips his arm under BURR'S and hauls him offstage, to the laughter of the CHORUS.*

Scene 4

    The WORKERS CHORUS *removes the long table and returns with the small one; also chairs and the podium.* MARSHALL *enters with his cane and the Bible and sets the Bible on the table.* BURR *enters with a bowl and a glass of wine; to make room for these on the table he sets the Bible on the floor.* THEO *brings his red coat, which she is sewing. The* CHORUS *brings in a flagpole, placing it to one side of the podium, the same as at the Inauguration. They comment as they work:*

CHORUS.
The year is 1807. Here we are—
Richmond, Virginia, where Burr is brought to trial.

CHORUS A.
This is no courthouse, it's a huge hall full
of frontier farmers, tradesmen, the idle rich—
Folks like yourselves: if there's a show, they'll watch.

CHORUS B *(pointing into the audience).*
Washington Irving's in town to report
Burr's trial for the papers in New York.

CHORUS A *(one asks, the other answers).*
Andrew Jackson cracks jokes in the steaming streets:
"What's worse 'n findin' bugs in yer marriage-bed?...
...Findin' a Burr in yer sheets!"

CHORUS B *(laughter among themselves).*
All are here for a view of history,
but we will see what we will see—

CHORUS A.
We *won't* see President Jefferson.
Justice Marshall tried but he can't make him
answer a subpoena *duces tecum.*

CHORUS B.
A second summons comes, he scarcely budges—

CHORUS A.
Which tells you what he thinks of judges!

CHORUS B.
Well, that's enough of our folderol—
You want to see what happens, and you shall.
But bear in mind, though it's hot as hell,
you won't find people sporting snowy wigs,
patting their powder, wiping white sweat, *etcetera*.
The court is uncomfortable, but informal.
Here you see Burr at his leisure,
sipping his soup and wine. His daughter
sews the sleeve of his velvet coat, while he
speaks with Justice Marshall, privately.

> *The CHORUS exits, left, and the door closes behind them.*

BURR.
Sir, you must know a little law.
Why can't I be free on bail?

MARSHALL.
Jefferson says you're guilty as the devil.
So the Senate has denied your right
of habeas corpus. You're *his* prisoner
until you go to the gallows, or acquit yourself.

BURR *(as THEO removes his dish and glass).*
I'll dance on the grave of that grey-faced fox.

> *BURR rises, picks up the Bible. THEO returns.*

THEO.
Papa, that Bible is too heavy for your dessert.

BURR *(setting the Bible on the table).*
It's more than I can digest.

THEO *(in a low voice as she watches MARSHALL).*
We have other food for thought.

BURR.
Speak up. My friend knows my failings.

THEO.
It's Blennerhassett's man, Mr. Love.
I met him coming to court today—
He tells me Maggie's had a baby boy.

BURR.
Love strikes again!
That's hardly an original story.
Does her hubby suspect that I'm the author?

THEO.
No, no, Blenny boasts like a fond father!

BURR.
I must pay him for our provisions
now that his home is gone.

THEO.
The island was overrun by militia men.
Their best livestock were butchered.
Before I fled with young Aaron
one man began to brain the sheep,
a sweating fellow swinging a mallet—

BURR *(interrupting)*.
And the whiskey cellar?

THEO.
Dry as the devil's eyes.
Every keg down the gullet.

BURR.
I weep to hear it.

THEO.
Now Maggie has her little lad to feed.

MARSHALL.
This means trouble, while the trial is in doubt.

THEO.
Only one man could harm us worse.

BURR.
They dare not drag their pet hog into court!

MARSHALL.
The prosecutor assures me
he'll question Wilkinson in the flesh.

BURR.
Will that fat fellow testify?
If I'm tarred with treason, the stuff sticks to him.

MARSHALL.
The President has pardoned him.

BURR.
Apparently, Tom pardons everyone but me.

THEO.
Papa, you pass so near his orbit
that you might dim his name.

BURR *(indicating the audience)*.
When this jury sets me free
my fame will eclipse
anyone who sits in the capital.

> BURR takes THEO'S hands. He's suddenly urgent, soft-spoken.

You understand because you're my own blood.
You know each breath is born to rise
above the gravity of laws—
How they weigh down our dreams,
these laws that we forge in fear, like chains.
Every link is an iron lock
hung on the heart. *This* is our folly,
Missy; people who dare not dream go mad!

> BURR walks THEO to a corner downstage, where she sits. MARSHALL remains behind the podium, the flag to his right. The Bible is on the table in front of the podium. LAWYER PERKINS enters and sits near the podium, while BURR stands opposite, leaving a chair for the witness. BURR and PERKINS address the audience, which is the jury.

MARSHALL.
Assisting the District Attorney,
Lawyer Perkins will address the jury.

PERKINS (*standing*).
Colonel Burr is charged with treason, for we claim
he plotted to seize the city of New Orleans.
The Colonel then might conquer Mexico
and with her gold reward his troops.
Wealthy, wined, well-armed, they return
to dismember our union. If any *one*
of these plots be proved, he's guilty of treason.

PERKINS pauses and looks over the audience.

You recall his heroism in the Revolution.
And to us lawyers he's a livin' legend.
We don't dare discredit him by discussin'
that fatal duel he fought one mornin'...
For Colonel Burr has been our Vice President,
the second citizen of our government.
How we wish his aim had been honorable!
But what Burr did in cold blood was no less
than the crime of Cassius. It calls forth
our wrath. The sentence shall be *Death*.

BURR.
How does our Constitution define treason?

PERKINS.
To wage war against this nation, or comfort our enemy.

BURR.
Are we are war?

PERKINS.
Sir?

BURR.
When the Congress does not declare a state of war
who's our enemy?
Anyone who frightens Jefferson?

PERKINS.
We'll waive that half of our definition.
Burr gave comfort to no one.

    Laughter from MARSHALL and THEO.

BURR *(wholly serious)*.
I claim protection under our Constitution.

PERKINS *(indignant)*.
Which you call a worthless piece of paper!

BURR.
Should the law protect only those people
who praise it? Soldiers stole my property!
Through dark woods and wild waters
my daughter and my little grandson fled
the abuse of your troops...

PERKINS.
Our prisoner claims he's a victim of persecution.
I'll show the reason for his occupation
of that island fortress. I call William Love...
We'll prove Burr brought men there to train for war.

    LOVE enters, lays his hand on the Bible, and sits down.

Mr. Love, you've sworn to tell us the truth.
Were you employed by Herman Blennerhassett
on his island in the Ohio River?

LOVE *(annoyed)*.
I was his man-servant, I lived there.

PERKINS.
Is it true a kiln was built, for dryin' corn?

LOVE.
Yes. I saw it.
He told me he was laying-in provision.

PERKINS.
More than enough to feed his family?

LOVE.
Enough to feed an army.

BURR *(turning away)*.
Or to feed other families? Poor people in need?

LOVE.
He said that you forbid families, sir.
Too cumbersome for quick maneuvers.
Every man a lone wolf like yourself, he said. *Sir.*

BURR.
Blenny wasn't as blind as I thought.

PERKINS.
Did an army of such men arrive?

BURR.
I object to the term *army*. It presumes
the intent of those men, which you haven't proved.

PERKINS *(slowly, patiently)*.
Did many men arrive? Were they given guns?

LOVE.
Yes.

BURR.
Come now, was every man given a gun?

LOVE.
There might have been more men than guns.

VOICE *(from the audience)*.
Did you see Burr among them?

LOVE.
Frequently.

VOICE *(from the audience)*.
Did you see men making bullets?

LOVE.
Yes, I saw them making many rounds.

BURR.
For what kind of guns? Hunting guns?

LOVE *(cheerfully)*.
That depends, *sir,* on what you're hunting.

    Laughter. MARSHALL raps for order with his cane.

BURR.
Love makes us laugh at our troubles.
Think now, when we last met,
were my guests equipped with bayonets?

LOVE.
Well now, I must say, I saw no bayonets.

BURR.
Then they could have been a hunting party?

PERKINS.
I object. That's speculation.

BURR.
But the witness may give us his opinion.
Were the men military, in their manner?
Or did they look like young gentlemen?

LOVE.
They might have passed for gentlemen, in *your* view.

    Laughter. MARSHALL again raps for order.

PERKINS *(quickly)*.
Your Honor, I've finished with this witness.

MARSHALL *(to Burr)*.
Do *you* still wish to question Mr. Love?

BURR *(drawn out, for effect)*.
Lord, no! For once in my life
I've had enough of Love...

    Laughter from THEO. WILLIAM LOVE exits.

VOICE *(from the audience)*.
Where's Wilkinson?

    GENERAL WILKINSON enters in full dress uniform, a sword worn at one side. A portly man with white hair and a florid face, he presents himself to all, a hand on the Bible. BURR ignores him.

THEO *(as Burr approaches)*.
Is this the hour of our doom?
Or fame?

BURR.
Missy, these few minutes are eternity for me.
If I can put our President in jail—

THEO *(in agreement)*.
Papa, he seizes your possessions, your weapons.
He maligns your name.
He plots against your rights as a free man!

BURR.
I'll replace Tom tomorrow by popular choice.
I'll be the Barabbas these people prefer
to their soft-spoken savior.

PERKINS *(to WILKINSON)*.
You're sworn to tell this court the truth?

WILKINSON *(as BURR returns)*.
This court, sir, and every soul on earth.

PERKINS.
You're General James Wilkinson, of the U.S. Army?

    BURR glares at WILKINSON then looks away from him.

WILKINSON.
I am.

PERKINS.
And you received a letter from Colonel Burr?

WILKINSON *(holding up the letter)*.
I have it here. He promises to lead
an unlawful army against Mexico.
Seizing New Orleans would be necessary.
I suppose that's why he wrote to *me*.

    PERKINS *hands the letter to* MARSHALL.

BURR.
Were you in command throughout that territory?

WILKINSON *(straining for modesty)*.
Second always to my Commander-in-Chief.

BURR.
And now you are its Governor...
Were you appointed by the President?

WILKINSON.
Yes, sir! I was.

BURR.
After you agreed to testify?

WILKINSON.
As I remember, perhaps my appointment came after.

BURR.
To obtain your testimony?

WILKINSON *(to MARSHALL)*.
Does that deserve a reply?

MARSHALL.
It requires one.

WILKINSON.
Then my answer is *No*.
But why am I questioned so?
I have nothing to hide.

BURR.
And so much hide in which to conceal it.

MARSHALL *(taking up the letter)*.
Certain words have been removed from this letter.

WILKINSON
I flaked them off with my pen-knife.

MARSHALL.
For what purpose?

WILKINSON.
For clearer reading.

>   *Laughter from THEO. PERKINS glares.*

BURR.
Tell us, sir...
Were you ordered to betray Colonel Burr?

WILKINSON.
I feel great delicacy about disclosing my orders.

BURR.
The whale has a delicate stomach.
Once it spit up a whole man, but that's an old tale.
Who ordered you to betray Colonel Burr?

WILKINSON *(after a long pause)*.
President Jefferson.

MARSHALL.
Produce the written order for this court.

WILKINSON.
I *won't* produce it. I'd rather rot in jail!

BURR.
I pray they don't crowd us in the same cell.

MARSHALL.
You will show us your order from the President.

WILKINSON *(brushing about his uniform).*
God Almighty! I discover I've made a mistake.
I have no order to seize Colonel Burr.
But I did believe I had an order.

BURR *(to audience).*
Did you ever see a weasel as wide as this fellow?

MARSHALL.
Colonel Burr claims that he wrote to you,
as a man in authority who endorsed his plan.
If you admit your approval, it could clear his name.

> WILKINSON *rises in outrage, draws his sword, and points it at* BURR.

WILKINSON *(shouting).*
Why, then I'd be guilty of his crime!
Sir, I've sworn my solemn oath.
For that scoundrel to declare
that I was aware of his treason
is fallow ground, without a grain of truth!

> PERKINS *pulls* WILKINSON *aside, lowers his sword, and leads him away.* WILKINSON *stomps from the courtroom and* PERKINS *returns.*

MARSHALL *(to the audience).*
Ladies and gentlemen of the jury,
your duty is clear in the case of Aaron Burr.
private citizens who wage war
commit treason under our Constitution.

> *Cries of a hostile crowd come from beyond the closed door upstage left, calling for* BURR *to be hanged. Then* MARSHALL *continues, despite the sound of someone pounding on the door.*

Often that term *treason*, like a fire bell,
has rung alarm in this courtroom.
But have you heard evidence of the deed?
Or was some lawless action only planned?
You see, we must have witnessed war
or the crime of plotting it cannot exist.

The green graveyards of our Revolution
remind us that war is a willing servant,
awaiting our summons, whenever required.

> *The crowd is suddenly quiet.*

But consider in your hearts: Was violence done?
Whose blood has been shed?
And where do the dead lie down?
It matters not if there was violent thought
or speech. Mere murmurs of unrest
won't trouble us. That day is past
when a tyrant might imprison citizens
without regard for their God-given rights—
When we must forfeit our lives, for our thoughts.

Either war was waged or it was not.

Now each one do your duty as you see it.

> *A working man, whose voice had been heard earlier calling questions from the audience, leaves the audience and comes onstage to speak for the jury.*

JUROR *(showing a piece of paper).*
Your Honor, we have our verdict.

MARSHALL.
You will please read it.

JUROR *(handing over the paper).*
I don't read, sir...So you do it?

MARSHALL *(reads the note in silence).*
You understand what this says?

JUROR.
It's *our* verdict. What we all say.

MARSHALL *(returning the note).*
Say it aloud then, for this court to hear.

JUROR (*slowly, carefully*).
Here's how it is, Your Honor...We regret...
we can't quite convict Aaron Burr
on the evidence brought before us.

BURR (*as THEO rushes to him*).
John, I object!
My good name must be washed clean.
The jury must say "Guilty" or "Not Guilty."

JUROR.
We've said what we mean.

MARSHALL.
I'm sure you have. Now you may leave,
with the thanks of the court.

> *The JUROR exits. MARSHALL continues, to the audience.*

Let the record read "Not guilty."
Colonel Burr did scheme against the country of his birth.
He did seduce our youth to support his plot.

> *He turns to BURR.*

You did demonstrate contempt for our laws
and worse contempt for our people.
Took up weapons to attack your own countrymen.
And now you want them to forgive you? No,
I'm satisfied this court has done
its duty by our Constitution.
I mean Mr. Jefferson has failed
to hang you with his own hands...So the law
of the people is upheld, though not their will.

BURR.
Is this how you keep faith with your friends?

MARSHALL.
Look, we laughed and schemed and drank together,
but this black robe has made me sober.
I supported you each time you sought the vote
of the people. To steal
power at gunpoint is another matter.

Aaron, as your friend, I might forgive you,
but the law overshadows my love.

BURR.
A dreary love it is! Listen,
I'm free!
I obey no law
that shrouds my liberty!

> *The crowd again is shouting, and pounding on the door.*

MARSHALL.
You're free to leave
while your neck's a normal size—
Or meet that mob
ready to stretch it with their rope.

> *LAWYER PERKINS exits with the Bible, as THEO brushes BURR'S coat, looking about. The crowd continues shouting.*

THEO.
Papa, it's horrid! Those howls—

BURR.
The squeals of swine.

THEO.
Damn them, the verdict's in. We've won!

> *As BURR exits, right, THEO shouts first at the crowd beyond the closed door, then at the audience.*

Papa is innocent, do you hear? Do you hear?

MARSHALL.
This court never said Burr wasn't at fault...

> *He swings his cane toward the audience.*

But these people could not determine his guilt.

> *The door flies open and the CHORUS, as the crowd, spills into the courtroom.*

CHORUS A.
Stretch his neck from the tallest tree!

CHORUS B.
Let him be; he's as good as dead.

CHORUS A *(to MARSHALL)*.
You set him free on a technicality.

CHORUS B *(to THEO)*.
We know he plotted to overthrow
our President...

CHORUS *(to all)*.
And the traitor breathes today
because he was brought to trial
before his crime made history. But where's Burr?

MARSHALL *(pointing with his cane)*.
As you see, he slipped your guard.
Burr understands the First Rule of Rebellion:
"He who hesitates is hanged."
He waits for his daughter outside the prison yard.

    The CHORUS drags in an effigy of Burr, including boots, red coat, and pistols, on a pole with a wide base.

THEO.
He should be here, to cheer his victory!

CHORUS.
This effigy will serve, it's a handsome fraud.
His hollow image, fit for hanging,
so you may have your hero to applaud.

    The CHORUS raises Burr's effigy beside the podium, at the same height as the U.S. flag on the opposite side. Lighting accentuates the flag and the effigy. THEO cries out, then she runs from the stage.

CHORUS.
He won his case in court, but Burr's no fool—
He knows from this day forth
his trial is held in the heart

of anyone who hears of his betrayal,
and no one in the land will take his part.

    MARSHALL exits, right, and the CHORUS exits, left. Spotlights remain on the flag and the effigy, hanging opposite each other, as all the other lights fade out.

Curtain

A DRAMA OF LIVING FORMS

A Drama of Living Forms

Spoken poetry, Garcia Lorca said, requires "a living body to interpret it." In the theater it provides, as he said of Spanish dance and the bullfight, "a drama of living forms." I think he presents a persuasive argument for the use of poetry in drama. In fact, the advantages of verse in the theater are so compelling to a writer that they overcome the most obvious disadvantage, the small chance of a box-office success.

But that risk of limited commercial prosperity didn't deter Ezra Pound from developing the tough, sinuous line of variable verse that he employed in *Women of Trachis*. And it hasn't prevented the popular and artistic success of *Blood Wedding, Murder in the Cathedral, J.B.*, or *Marat/Sade*; all offer examples of what can be accomplished in dramatic verse, though each employs a distinctly different verse line.

In writing *The Best Blood of the Country*, I wanted a flexible accentual line suitable to speech rhythms which change as the dramatic tension increases or lessens. I think the line should impose its cadence on the audience, and challenge the audience to be alert for the emphasis upon words and phrases which that cadence will assert. I want a line which is heard and felt, not a self-effacing line that might pass unnoticed, disguised as prose. In notes I'd written to myself while working on the script, there is the reminder that these three-, four-, and five-stress lines must carry or counterpoint the speech rhythms, to create the appropriate tension of each moment. The rhythm is to *in*form the speech with its tensions, helping to build the dramatic situation. The rhythmic line is never an adornment, it's an essential element in the drama.

Like rhythm, rhyme is recurrent, so its appearance in a pattern suggests design; it suggests that the mind of a character is shaping the material given to it. Since the Workers Chorus provides us the voice of the public, its four members speak at times in rhyme, suggesting the coming together of their thoughts to form a common opinion.

I think the bonding qualities of sound can contribute to dramatic meaning, whether in assonance, alliteration, rhyme, or even an interlocking rhyme which, through their speech, joins one character to another.

In contrast to this joining effect, the doggerel of the Workers Chorus draws us outside the dramatic moment, to consider it from a public viewpoint. Theirs is a verse of obvious meter and sound. As a means of distancing, it reminds us that we're hearing the voice of popular opinion. When the Chorus comments on the actions of Burr or anyone else, it's not with the scrutiny of a camera close-up. They give a panoramic effect, showing an individual's deeds in the midst of the larger human community. A major concern of this drama is the struggle between the individual and the community, and I'd like to see that concern brought out by any of the elements of writing or stagecraft which can help to express it.

Poetry is effective in drama because it gives emphasis to statement, imagery, cadence, and feeling, for the performer who speaks it, and it deepens the attention of the audience. After all, it's for these, simultaneously, that you write: for the character, for the performer who will play that character, and for the immediate moment in the story, which is the eternal present that engages the author and the audience.

Drama embodies such moments in characters involved in the stories of their lives. Which are also the stories of *our* lives. And spoken poetry, within the dramatic structure of a story, enhances our involvement in that story.

Lorca urged that poetry in the theater can raise up among us a living body alert to language and action, the drama of living forms. The point is not that this alert state, this awareness, is larger than life—it isn't—but that life is larger than we had thought

It's true that a genre which can so fully engage us must also run the risk of failure. And yet if we're fortunate, as writers or as audience, it makes more vivid the imagined life and so it transforms us. How can we fail to accept an opportunity like that? The alternative is silence or sameness, in ourselves and in our art. I think the risk is always worth taking.

G.K.